To Serena

...his
...ect

Fanta + Barney
xx
XMAS 2005

the old age of el magnifico

# Doris Lessing

# the old age of el magnifico

**Flamingo**
*An Imprint of HarperCollinsPublishers*

Flamingo
An Imprint of HarperCollins*Publishers*
77–85 Fulham Palace Road,
Hammersmith, London W6 8JB

www.**fire**and**water**.com

Flamingo is a registered trade mark of
HarperCollins*Publishers* Limited

Published by Flamingo 2000
9 8 7 6 5 4 3 2

Copyright © Doris Lessing 2000

Doris Lessing asserts the moral right to
be identified as the author of this book

A catalogue record for this book
is available from the British Library

Illustration of cat on piii
© Elizabeth Blackadder

ISBN 0 00 226200 2

Set in Perpetua by
Rowland Phototypesetting Ltd,
Bury St Edmunds, Suffolk

Printed and bound in Great Britain

All rights reserved. No part of this publication may be
reproduced, stored in a retrieval system, or transmitted,
in any form or by any means, electronic, mechanical,
photocopying, recording or otherwise, without the prior
permission of the publishers.

the old age of el magnifico

A WEEK BEFORE our cat had his front leg or, rather, his whole haunch taken off, he raced down seven flights of stairs, then bang *crash* through the cat door and along the garden path to the fence at the end, to see off the enormous grey tom who visits our gardens from across the reservoir. His screeching howl of defiance was such that when he returned, calm, victorious, to my bed at the very top of the house and sat looking over his territory, emptied of all cats but himself, and then over the fence to the wide green field that is the reservoir — the Victorians put their water underground — I said to him, as usual shaken by that voice of his, But Good

God Butchkin! That is the most intolerable yowl.

Butchkin? Not The Magnificence? It was like this. Seventeen springs ago a cat called Susie gave birth to her kittens in the roof space near my room. She was a friendly civilised cat, so she must have had a good home, but had lost it, and was living rough, sometimes fed and sometimes not by the ladies at the lunch centre, had given birth to at least two sets of kittens anywhere she could find a corner – once it was under a lorry – and those kittens had not survived. She was not an old cat, but she was tired and frightened. Mother cats who have had many litters, not having been rescued by kindly owners with an operation, may acknowledge their enormous belly that squirms and bulges because of the vivacious load inside, with unmistakable weariness. 'Oh *no*, do I have to go through all that again?' This cat was given food, safety, a place in the roof where no other cat could even approach, but she was a reluctant mother, though dutiful.

When kittens first open their little hazy bluish eyes and see the humans towering over them they may hiss and defy, before becoming companionable cats, but among Susie's kittens was one black and white scrap who opened his eyes, saw me, climbed unsteadily off the old blanket on to the floor . . . then on to my leg . . . up my leg . . . my arm . . . my shoulder . . . clinging on with his tiny prickles of claws, got under my chin and cuddled there, purring. This was love, and for life. He was the biggest kitten, the boss kitten, and from the start took command of them all, even washed and chastised them, while his big mother lay stretched out, watching. He was like a father to those kittens, or even a mother. Susie did not seem to care for him more than the others, or disapprove of his bossiness.

There is a mystery about the birth of those kittens. There were seven. One, a white kit — and it is painful to think how beautiful a cat he would have been — she pushed out of the nest, and it was found dead a couple of days later. Unless it was born dead, unlikely, since all the others were so lively. And she pushed out another, too, a little tabby. I left it for half a day, cold and unfed, thinking I must stop my sentimentality, grieving about nature's choices: if she had thrown him out then who was I etc. but

# the old age of el magnifico

I could not bear it, hearing his feeble mews, and I put him back among the others, and there were six thriving kits. Susie, then, had an ambiguous attitude to those kittens. Seven, she had clearly thought, were too many, and even six were. She had not been prepared to mother more than five kittens, and certainly when the six were rampaging around my room one could see her point.

I am saying that this cat could count, and if she was not thinking, one, two, three, four, five, then she knew the difference between five and seven. Most scientists would dispute this, I'm pretty sure. That is, as scientists they would, but as owners of cats, probably not. It is interesting, watching a scientist friend talking about cat capacities that he would officially deny. His cat is always in the window waiting for him to come home, he says, but wearing his other hat, says animals have no sense of time, they live in an eternal now. He may go on to say that if he is not expected home, the cat is not there, but this takes him into regions he finds intolerable. The fact is, any observant careful cat owner knows more about cats than the people who authoritatively study them. Serious information about the ways of cats, and other animals, is often in magazines with names like *Cat News*, or *Pussy Pals*, and no scientist would dream of reading them. There you will find tales like this: a farm cat, whose kittens as they were born were always taken from her, leaving one, surprised her owners after many litters by giving birth to only one kitten. Tactful of her, they thought, but she had carried four kittens up to the attic, one by one, and there she went to feed them, secretly, spending her time ostensibly with the one permitted kitten. The farmer and his wife heard the scampering upstairs, discovered their cat's clever deception – and it would be nice to think they found a good home for the kittens and had their poor cat spayed.

Susie seemed pleased enough to find a willing helper in her bossy kitten, but there was some ambivalence there too. This kitten's weak point was that he often coughed, or seemed to find an irritant in his throat. His mother then went to him, sat, and took his neck and lower head in her big jaws. If she tightened those jaws she would kill him, but no, she held him, for half a minute, a minute, and I wondered if there was a nerve or a pressure point, and she knew how to stop his spluttering and coughing. He did stop, not at once. Later, when he was grown, and he coughed, I did what Susie had done, clamp my fingers as she had her jaws. He does stop coughing, after a bit.

This kitten was bigger than the others, and we called him Butch in joke, because it was ridiculous, this tiny thing, this blob of a kitten, becoming the kindly tyrant of the nursery. We intended to drop the name, this boring unimaginative name, that half the male cats in the country get called, and dogs too, Butch, Big Butch, but the name stuck, though softened, first because of his kitten status, to Butchkin, and then Pushkin, or Pusskin, Pusscat, Pushka – all the variations on the ppsssk psssh puss sounds that for some reason seem to fit with the reality of Cat. You would never call a cat Rover, though he may wander further than a dog. The honorifics this cat had earned, El Magnifico being only one, are for special occasions, as when he is being introduced. 'What is he called?' 'General Pinknose the Third' – (for he is not the first cat whose tiny pink nose in some lights and poses seems gently to mock the pretensions of the imposing beast. What a fine cat, says the visitor, disconcerted, imagining that we call the full name into the garden, or even 'General! Where are you?' There are some names that refer not to this particular cat, but to the owners' history with cats. But El Magnifico suits him best, suits him, because he truly is such a magnificent cat.

Doris Lessing

He was a lithe and handsome black and white young cat, and he and his brother, a tabby, a tiger, were a fine pair, but El Magnifico had to grow into his full glory, dramatic black and white, and then you thought, awed, this creature, this magnificence, has evolved from basic moggy, from your ordinary London cat-stuff, the product of hundreds of years of haphazard matings – or at least that have no concern at all for pedigree – between run-of-the-mill puss and cat-as-catch-can, between black cats, and black and white cats, and tabbies, and marmalades and tortoiseshells and the result is just an ordinary black and white cat – and what could be more common than that? And yet, at his best, visitors could walk into a room where he lay stretched out, an enormous lordly beast, a harlequinade of black and white, and stop and exclaim, 'What a marvellous cat', and then, unable to believe this beast was just mogg-stuff, 'But *what* is he?' 'Oh, he's just an ordinary cat.'

Fourteen years old, and in full health, and there was a lump on his shoulder. To the vet he went. Cancer of the bone of his shoulder. Now the whole front leg had to come off, that is, the whole haunch, shoulder and all.

The humans went into shock. *This* cat a three-legged cat? Surely he would not endure the ignominy of it. But the day was fixed, and El Magnifico, complaining at the top of his voice, for he has never been one to suffer in silence, was driven to a famous cat surgeon, and there left in the care of a nurse. We were assured he would manage perfectly well with three legs. He must stay several days with them to recuperate. This in itself must be hard for him to bear, for he had lived his entire life in this house, where he was born. Out of it he wailed and mourned. It must be confessed that there is a bit of a babyish streak in our cat. Compare him with his mother Susie, whose hard life had made her a brave and stoical beast. Or the cat we nursed for a couple of years, Rufus, who, to survive at all had to be cunning and clever. No, as in many people, here was a contradiction: Butchkin was, still is, proud, intelligent, the most intuitive cat I've known, but like some people who have never had to fight for their food or their place in the world, he has a soft place in him. And, too, inside that great handsome beast lurks another surprising persona: he is sometimes histrionic, an actor of the old-fashioned kind, all the stops out, to make outrageous emotional scenes. When he feels he is being ignored, not given his due, he lets us know it, and sometimes his humans, overcome with laughter, have to go hastily into another room, for he is so funny, but of course we would not let him see us laugh, he would never forgive the insult.

When we left him at the cat surgeon's, his miaowing was certainly not for effect. He had had to starve, and then he had injections, and then a large area of him was shaved. We heard the operation was a success, and he was now a three-legged cat. That morning he had lain stretched out on my bed in the sun, one long elegant paw negligently over the other, and I had stroked the leg that would soon not be there, and caressed the paw that curled up to hold my finger, when I inserted it, as I had when he was a kitten, the tiny paw crisping around the tip of my little finger. It was unendurable that the furry limb would be thrown away into an incinerator.

We kept telephoning, we were reassured, yes, he was eating, yes, he was fine, but he must stay with them for some days. And then they rang to say they thought it best if we took him home, for he was not doing well in confinement, was trying to climb the walls of his cage and – yes, we could imagine what earsplitting yowls were doing to the nerves of the nurses.

## the old age of el magnifico

They told us we must put him in a room with the door tight shut, and not let him out for a week, because of the stitches in that dreadful wound, and because of infection. We brought him home and he cried all the way. He was a shocked cat. His friends, his family, and particularly the friend on whose bed he slept, and who had adored him all his life, had put him in a basket, which he hated, and about which he had always strongly expressed his views, and then he was driven he didn't know where, but it was a longer journey than he had ever endured, and there he had been surrounded by strange voices and smells, and carried down to an underground place smelling strongly of unfriendly cats, and there he had been shut in, his family suddenly not there, and needles were stuck into him, and they cut off his fur, and then he woke up, very sore, very weak, and one of his legs had gone, and he kept falling on his face when he tried to walk. And now these so-called friends were carrying him upstairs in his own house, the stairs he had been rushing up and down all his life, and, as if they had not betrayed him, were petting him and caressing his good shoulder. At the top of the house, before we could shut the door on him, he tore himself out of the arms that held him, and flung himself down all seven flights of stairs, rolling, falling, jumping, getting down them any way he could. At the cat flap into the garden we caught up with him, and carried him into the garden, and put him on a blanket under a bush. He was afraid of being shut up again, imprisoned. And though this great wound was only a couple of days old, he was creeping about the garden, and even went through the fence to next door, and then to the fence at the bottom of the garden. It looked as if he was making sure he could escape if he had to, away from the people who had inflicted these terrible insults, and this wound. We brought him in at night, shut him up, fed him, gave him medicines, talked to him, but he wanted to be out, and for the next few days every morning I carried him to his bush, with a bowl of water, and went out to commiserate, and stroke and reassure. He was polite. One day, hearing a howl from him I had never heard before, I looked out and he was balancing on his three legs, and he was lifting his head to howl. This was not one of his histrionic efforts, but from the heart, a cry of anguish, and when he had dispersed the tension, the pain, the bewilderment, the disgrace of his absent leg, he lay down for a while, but then got himself up and cried. It made my blood run cold, made me frantic with frustration, because he was living through a nightmare and he could not understand it and I could not explain it to him.

'Cat, if we had not done that to you you would be dead in a couple of months – do you understand that?' No, of course not. 'Cat, because of the amazing cleverness of the human race you are alive and not dead, as you soon would be, in your natural state.'

I brought him up to sleep on my bed, and soon he was crawling up the stairs himself. One night I was awake and reading, and he was asleep, and then he started up, as we may do, out of sleep, out of a dream, and he let out a frightened cry, looking about him, not knowing where he was – perhaps he was back in that prison cage – but then the nightmare faded, and he lay down quietly and looked out into the night beyond the big windows. I stroked, and he did not purr, I stroked, I stroked, and at last he purred. Several times he came awake suddenly out of a nightmare, and then – time passed, he did not, I think, have bad dreams. (That cats do dream, science has confirmed.)

But I was remembering an earlier wrong. When he and his brother were the right age, young cats but not fully grown, they were taken to be 'neutered', and brought back home, and put, each one, on a low soft cushion, where they lay stretched out, their tails flowing out behind them, and this cat, my Butchkin, my magnifico, lifted his head and looked at me and never has anything been clearer than that long deep look: You are my friend, and yet you have done this to me. For under his tail was a bloody wound, and his little furry cat balls had gone, leaving an empty sac. Yes of course it had to be done: but it is no use saying that a neutered cat lives longer than a 'whole' cat, does not roam the neighbourhood fighting and getting more and more beaten up and battered, because the moment when you agree that a 'whole' cat must be cut and diminished to live ball-less . . . well, it is a bad one, and acknowledgement of the commonsense of the thing does not diminish the basic guilt: This cat is less of a cat than he was and it is my fault. The long long look, reproach, enquiry, '*Why*, when you are my friend?'

Soon, just as the vet had said he would, he was up and down those stairs, springing lightly on one paw, he was on and off the bed and the sofas, he was managing everything easily, but he was not the same in himself. He had been humiliated, his pride, that most sensitive of a cat's organs, had been hurt. His dignity was hurt because he hobbled, and surely he must be remembering, as we did, his lordly careless stroll every time he miscalculated and fell on his nose. What had been his advantage, his size, was now against him, for his remaining front leg, that slender limb, was taking all his weight, and the shoulder joint had become swollen and knobbly. The vet said there was water there, under the flesh and if there was something bad hidden deep in the joint, then it would take its time. There was only a ten per cent chance of the cancer returning.

Nearly three years have passed. The cat has had that extra life. He has done well. His coat is glossy, he is a handsome elderly cat, with a sprinkle of grey on one ear. His eyes are bright. He manages his restricted life with that curious assessment of possibilities and risks that you see in people who lack a limb, are disabled: I first watched it in my father, who had lost his leg in the war.

But El Magnifico is lonely. He has been used to a household of cats. His mother's six kittens filled the whole house with their games before off they went to their homes. One, Charlie, stayed for a time. He was a handsome rakish cat, the tiger, with all a younger brother's characteristics, and watching him with big, calm, dominating Butchkin was better than a textbook on sibling relationships. Then there was Rufus, who was so ill, and who needed so much attention, but he tried to be the boss cat, and when Butchkin wouldn't have that the two male cats led parallel lives, ignoring each other. Yet when Rufus got too ill to live, Butchkin missed him, called for him, looked for him everywhere in the house and garden. Cats used to drop in. One, whom we fed for a year or so, because he clearly had a bad home, and preferred ours, was run over and had a serious operation involving two cat doctors and two nurses, because the car had pushed his abdominal organs up into his chest cavity. He was found a good home and lived another five years. One we called The Pirate, because he always came into our house like a raider, he had obviously been badly fed, because he could never pass food without eating it all up, every bit, was always hungry. Butchkin used to sit and watch him eat – and eat. Butchkin has never gone hungry, does not know what it is to think there might not be another meal after this one, and so he eats moderately, may decide to leave a plateful of food altogether, or may eat only half. This enormous cat, this great heavy beast has never been a good eater: it is his genes, his mother was a big bulky cat.

But now no cats drop in and out, climbing

up the lilac tree at the back of the house to visit, or to find a mouthful to eat, or a bowl of water. Because these days we have warmer weather, dryer weather, cats are often in search of water, and the bowl I put down on my front steps is visited by cats locked out of their homes during the day, or who are out on their investigations. There are no cats now who treat our home as theirs, there is only this crippled cat in the house and surely that is strange? Why don't they come in and out as they used to? The cat doctor said our cat's main problem would be other cats, because he could not defend himself, with only one paw. But he misses them.

He goes out into the garden and sits calling, calling . . . this is a different tone from the ones he uses with us. It is cajoling, canoodling, intimate. Next door is a young female cat who distresses her owner because she hunts black-birds and robins. She is far from beautiful, or even pretty. Her fur is rough, of a brownish colour, and she is muscled and compact. She has no grace or charm, but she is a deadly hunt-ress, and her swift movement towards her prey is like a snake's, smooth and fast. Of course we think she is not good enough for our handsome cat, but he wants her to be his friend, and sits calling, facing her house, then calling again, but she does not come, and so he brings himself clumsily through the cat door and heaves himself up the stairs. She is probably thinking, And why should I bother myself with that old crippled cat?

One afternoon I stood on the balcony and

observed this scene. Our cat is in the garden, calling, and next door's cat comes through the fence, but not looking at him. She walks indifferently past him. He makes small friendly noises, the same he uses to greet us. She walks on and through the fence on the other side. He follows, getting himself with difficulty through a small gap in the fence. She positions herself under the birch tree on the other side of that garden, facing him, but looking past him. He cautiously sits a few paces off. The two cats sit on, in some sort of communion. Then our cat tries his luck, moving carefully a few cat-paces closer. She hastily moves some distance away. He sits balancing himself, on his front leg and his backside. She licks herself a little. There is no coquetry in this honest young cat, she disdains

27

female wiles, quite unlike Grey Cat, whose life is such a long way in the past; she flirted and enticed and seduced humans as well as male cats. Butchkin continues to watch her. He then makes another move, not directly towards her, but off at an angle, and sits again, in fact nearer to her. She does not react. They sit on, she licking herself, or staring around, or putting out a paw to touch a beetle or something near her on the earth. He miaows softly, once, twice. No response from her. Then, after perhaps fifteen minutes, she walks past him, quite close, and sits near him, but with her back to him, looking into the wild part of the garden. He changes position to sit looking after her. He miaows again, inviting, enticing. She deliberately strolls into the wild garden where she becomes invisible, though the grasses wave where she is moving through them. She jumps up on to the fence, where he used to sit watching the squirrels and the birds, but he can't reach it now. Then she is off on to the great green plain of the reservoir grass, which has been newly cut. He calls after her, and then comes in, slowly up the stairs . . . they are getting hard for him, our flights and flights of stairs.

He had to go up and down them to use the garden to pee and defecate, and I did wonder if he would like a box, but felt this independent cat might find that insulting. Then it became clear that it was getting too much for him, and so now there is a cat box. Sometimes he does try to go out, but it hurts his shoulder, so knotted and swollen.

Immediately after his leg came off, when he defecated, his muscles tensed and worked under the smooth black slopes of his hide where his front shoulder was as he tried to scratch dirt over the mess. He went on, then looked to see what was happening, tried again, those muscles that had once moved the leg hard at work. And then – he looked foolish and embarrassed. He gave me a look as if to say he hoped I hadn't noticed the foolish effort. He stopped trying to cover his mess. Now he takes a long time positioning himself on his three legs, making sure of his balance.

His favourite place is a low sofa in the living room. Easy to step up and step down. There is, too, a low pallet near a radiator and there he places himself so that his painful shoulder

# the old age of el magnifico

gets the heat directly on it. Once he always slept on my bed, but there are two narrow and steep flights of stairs, and he does not come up them now. I miss him. No longer do I wake to find him stretched out, gazing into the night, his yellow eyes gleaming, or hear his little friendly sounds that accompany my days, as I go into a room or leave it. What a repertoire he has, the purrs and half purrs of welcome, the calls of welcome, the small grunt that is the acknowledgment of a situation, or a thankyou, or a warning, I am here, be careful, mind my shoulder. Sometimes what he says is not so pleasant. He will sit in front of me, look hard at me, and then let out a series of angry miaows, on one note. An accusation? I don't know.

When he was a young cat I would wake to

find him awake and then, seeing that I was, he would walk up the bed, lie down on my shoulder, put his paws around my neck, lay his furry cheek against my cheek, and give that deep sigh of content you hear from a young child when he is at last lifted up into loving arms. And I heard myself sigh in response. Then he purred and purred, until he was asleep in my arms.

What a luxury a cat is, the moments of shocking and startling pleasure in a day, the feel of the beast, the soft sleekness under your palm, the warmth when you wake on a cold night, the grace and charm even in a quite ordinary workaday puss. Cat walks across your room, and in that lonely stalk you see leopard or even panther, or it turns its head to acknowledge you and the yellow blaze of those eyes tells you what an exotic visitor you have here, in this household friend, the cat who purrs as you stroke, or rub his chin, or scratch his head.

The room below my bedroom has a bed, but it is a high bed, and a ramp of piled cushions, and blankets lets him easily get up and down off it. His range is now the living room, with trips to the kitchen and the little flat roof outside it, and to the floor above, where the dirt box waits for him on the landing.

He likes to be brushed slowly all over, and carefully, for the fur on the side where his front paw used to be gets rough and knotted. He likes to be kneaded and massaged, and to have his spine rubbed down, neck to tail, with my hand held hard. I wash his ears for him, and his eyes, for one paw does not do as good a job as two.

And he licks my hand, which for a moment or two does become a paw, so that I can rub it over the eye on the side he can't reach, again and again, for his spit, like ours, is healing and keeps the eye healthy.

Sometimes, if he has lain too long on the sofa, he can get down off it only with difficulty because he has stiffened up, the way I do, from sitting still, and then he does not even hobble, but crawls painfully, letting out a frustrated miaow, to his other place, where the radiator heat will loosen his old bones.

He is not doing badly, this old cat, with his three legs, and people coming into the room stop and exclaim, What a magnificent cat! – but when he gets up and hobbles away they are silent, particularly if they have seen him as a young cat step proudly out of a room, or lying on top of the basket – where he can no longer jump up – his two paws crossed negligently in front of him, his tail flowing down, his calm, deep eyes.

When you sit close to a cat you know well, and put your hand on him, trying to adjust to the rhythms of his life, so different from yours, sometimes he will lift his head and greet you with a soft sound different from all his other sounds, acknowledging that he knows you are trying to enter his existence. He looks at you with those eyes of his that continually adjust to changes in light, you look at him, your hand resting lightly. . . If a cat has nightmares then he must also dream as pleasantly and interestingly as we do. Perhaps his dreams could take

him to places I know in dreams, but I have
never met him there. I dream of cats often, cats
and kittens too, and I have responsibilities for
them, for dreams of cats are always reminders
of duty. The cats need feeding, or need shelter.
If our dream worlds are not the same, cats and
humans, or seem not to be, then when he sleeps
where does he travel?

He likes it when we sit quietly together. It
is not an easy thing, though. No good sitting
down by him when I am rushed, or thinking
about what I should be doing in the house or
garden or of what I should write. Long ago,
when he was a kitten, I learned that this was a
cat who demanded your full attention, for he
knew when my mind wandered, and it was no
use stroking him mechanically, my thoughts

elsewhere, let alone taking up a book to read. The moment I was no longer with him, completely thinking of him, then he walked off. When I sit down to be with him, it means slowing myself down, getting rid of the fret and the urgency. When I do this – and he must be in the right mood too, not in pain or restless – then he subtly lets me know he understands I am trying to reach him, reach cat, essence of cat, finding the best of him. Human and cat, we try to transcend what separates us.